DISCARDED

N 74-10284

Tebbel, John William, 1912–

The Battle of Fallen Timbers, August 20, 1794; President Washington secures the Ohio Valley, by John Tebbel. Illustrated with photos. and contemporary prints. New York, F. Watts, 1972.

87 p. illus. 23 cm. (A Focus book)

SUMMARY: Examines the events leading to the Battle of Fallen Timbers in 1794 which ended Indian and British control of the Ohio Valley.

Bibliography: p. 81.

1. U. S.—History—Constitutional period, 1789–1809. 2. Ohio Valley — History — To 1795. I. Title.

E313.T4   977'.02   76-188480
ISBN 0-531-02457-1   MARC

Library of Congress   72 [4]   AC

THE BATTLE OF FALLEN TIMBERS,
AUGUST 20, 1794

After the American Revolution ended, one of the most difficult problems the new nation faced was keeping peace with the Indians, particularly in the rich Ohio Valley. There the westward tide of settlers encountered not only powerful Indian tribes but also the British, who refused to give up the key forts which gave them control of the fur trade. Against the Indians and their British allies, President George Washington sent, first, General Josiah Harmar, who was badly defeated. Then Washington chose General Arthur St. Clair, who suffered one of the worst defeats in American military history at the hands of the great Indian war chief and orator, Little Turtle. But with Little Turtle deposed by jealous chiefs, the Indians could not withstand the third and decisive campaign mounted by General Anthony Wayne. He shattered their forces at the Battle of Fallen Timbers in August, 1794, ending Indian and British control of the Ohio Valley forever.

☆　☆

PRINCIPALS

GEORGE WASHINGTON, first President of the United States.

HENRY KNOX, Secretary of War.

BREVET BRIGADIER GENERAL JOSIAH HARMAR, leader of the first campaign.

MAJOR GENERAL ARTHUR ST. CLAIR, governor of the Northwest Territory and ranking general of the army, leader of the second campaign.

GENERAL ANTHONY WAYNE, the hero of Stony Point, who led the Battle of Fallen Timbers.

LITTLE TURTLE, leader of the Miami Indians and their allies.

A FOCUS BOOK

The Battle of
Fallen Timbers,
August 20, 1794

President Washington Secures the Ohio Valley

by John Tebbel

*illustrated with photographs
and contemporary prints*

Franklin Watts, Inc. / New York / 1972

The authors and publishers of the Focus Books wish to acknowledge the helpful editorial suggestions of Professor Richard B. Morris.

Cover photo courtesy *Charles Phelps Cushing*. Photo on title page (courtesy *The Bettmann Archive*) shows General Anthony Wayne and his men watching the Indians advance at Fallen Timbers, 1794.

Library of Congress Cataloging in Publication Data

Tebbel, John William, 1912-
    The Battle of Fallen Timbers, August 20, 1794.

    (A Focus book)
    SUMMARY: Examines the events leading to the Battle of Fallen Timbers in 1794 which ended Indian and British control of the Ohio Valley.
    Bibliography: p.
    1. U. S.–History–Constitutional period, 1789-1809–Juvenile literature. 2. Ohio Valley–History–To 1795–Juvenile literature. [1. U. S.–History–Constitutional period, 1789-1809. 2. Ohio Valley–History–To 1795] I. Title.
E313.T4   977'.02   76-188480
ISBN 0-531-02457-1

Contents

A New Nation   3

General Harmar's Expedition   13

St. Clair Takes the Field   20

Little Turtle's Campaign   26

President Washington's Defense   31

Congress Takes Action   37

Anthony Wayne Takes Command   41

A Council Leads to War   47

Wayne Begins His March   53

Little Turtle's Downfall   57

The Battle of Fallen Timbers   63

The Treaty of Greenville   71

Selected Bibliography   81

Index   83

THE BATTLE OF FALLEN TIMBERS,
AUGUST 20, 1794

A New Nation

As the last echo of the guns at Yorktown died away in the soft Virginia air, a great stirring swept across what had once been His Majesty's colonies in America. The Revolution was over, and a new nation was born. The British band played a popular tune, "The World Turn'd Upside Down," when the victorious General George Washington met his defeated British foe on the day of the official surrender. Now the colonies would no longer be the overseas possessions of Great Britain, but a nation of their own — to be called the United States of America.

In their happy belief that the war was ended — the siege of Charleston would continue for a year and a treaty would not be signed until September, 1783—a great many Americans must have thought their troubles were over. They were, in fact, just beginning.

Three major problems had to be faced immediately. One was how to devise a satisfactory system for ownership of the land that now opened up before the westward-moving settlers. Another was how to create a form of government strong enough to hold together the differing kinds of people who now called themselves Americans. The third problem was how to keep peace with the Indians in the region.

[3]

This engraving shows the British surrendering to Washington after their defeat at Yorktown. (Library of Congress)

In 1787, the Continental Congress had named the region east of the Mississippi River, north of the Ohio River, west of Pennsylvania, and south and west of the Great Lakes as the Northwest Territory. The ordinance provided that the territory would be divided into states, no more than five and no less than three. It also guaranteed religious freedom and the prohibition of slavery in the area. The first governor of the Northwest Territory was Arthur St. Clair.

It was the third major problem — how to keep peace with the Indians — that proved the hardest of all to solve. As far as the Indians were concerned, the end of the Revolution and the Treaty of 1783 settled nothing. Those in the Ohio Valley, especially, were bitter. It was *their* lands that the British and Americans had fought over, just as the British and French had fought over them only a few years before. The Indians had seen what the white man's war did to the noble Iroquois nation, in upstate New York. This once-mighty confederacy, known as the Six Nations, had been split, humbled, and removed from its former position of power.

In the Ohio Valley, then, there was little love among the Indians for the new nation and little trust of the new President, George Washington, who was not known for his love of red men. There was not much more admiration for the British either. However, those settlers from England who had lost the war had no intention of losing what they could get out of the peace.

What the British wanted was control of the fur trade they had enjoyed for so long. The means of control was a group of forts called the Northwest Posts. They stretched like a string of strategic pearls along the border with Canada, and their high palisades looked out over the water routes that led to the fur country. There were the forts at Dutchmen's Point and Point-au-Fer, on Lake Champlain; Oswegatchie and Oswego, at the eastern end of Lake Ontario;

[5]

and those at Niagara, Detroit, and the Straits of Mackinac, controlling the Great Lakes.

At these posts the merchants who were involved in the fur trade disposed of the goods they sold or traded to the Indians, and the intrepid adventurers who paddled their way into the interior unloaded rich cargoes of pelts. There were middlemen there, too, who imported goods from Montreal and sold them to the traders. At forts like Detroit and Mackinac, the ships that sailed the lakes unloaded goods to be sold to and traded with the Indians. Canoes took these goods to the tribes far away, deep in the forests.

Both the British and the Canadians were making an excellent profit from the fur trade, as they had before the Revolution. By controlling the forts they were almost able to exclude American traders.

According to the terms of the Treaty of 1783, British troops in the forts were supposed to evacuate them with all reasonable speed. But the British and the Canadians dragged their heels. They did not want to lose control of the fur trade, and they were afraid that with American troops in the forts, Canada itself would be threatened. The British government was no longer in a position to maintain these garrisons; it was up to the Canadians. Their governor-general, Frederick Haldimand, refused, however, to surrender the Northwest Posts.

But how could a nation occupy another nation's territory, acquired by treaty after a victorious war? The British ministers declared that the individual states had violated a section of the Treaty of 1783, forbidding the states to do anything that might prevent merchants and traders from recovering lawful debts. Until British traders could remove their goods, said the government, England would remain in possession of the Northwest Posts.

Early fur-trading post in the Northwest. (Charles Phelps Cushing)

While the Americans debated how they might counter this move, Governor-General Haldimand made another one. He realized that the key to holding the forts lay in persuading the Indians to ally themselves with the British, as many had done during the Revolution. Therefore, he began to fashion a confederation of tribes in the Ohio Valley. The alliance would be large enough to keep out the swarming tide of American settlers pouring into the valley and, at the same time, force the United States to give the whole region to the Indians as a buffer state, under British protection.

By 1788, Haldimand and his aides — men like the Tory commander of New York State, Sir John Johnson, and influential Indian leaders like Mohawk chief Joseph Brant — had succeeded in creating a powerful Indian alliance, among them Iroquois, Wyandots, Shawnees, Delawares, Miamis, Ottawas, Chippewas, and Potawatomis. These tribes vowed not to cede any more land to the United States unless the whole confederacy consented. They repudiated their previous treaties with the United States and declared that an Indian buffer state must be created between the Americans and the British, with the Ohio River as the border.

This clever plan failed because the Indians fell prey once more to the old curse that had prevented their every previous attempt to present a united front to the advancing white nations: they could not agree among themselves.

Some of the chiefs decided to press the Americans for a treaty that would give them the entire Ohio country. When the tribes discussed this idea, the Shawnees, Kickapoos, and Miamis asserted that the Ohio River must be the boundary. But the Wyandots, Delawares, and Senecas, who had had more experience with the white men, argued that such a demand would only lead to war, and they were against it.

Chippewa Indian girls harvesting wild rice. (The American Museum of Natural History)

Mohawk chief Joseph Brant. (The Bettmann Archive)

Brant vainly tried to work out a compromise before the chiefs met with agents of the United States at Fort Harmar in January, 1789, but his efforts only seemed to split the disputing chiefs even further apart. The American negotiator, Arthur St. Clair, took full advantage of their disagreement. Aggressively, he dictated a treaty worse than the one the Indians already lived under. Disheartened by this maneuver, and quarreling as much as ever, the chiefs slipped away from Fort Harmar and disappeared into the wilderness.

If all that was needed to set off this tinderbox was a lighted match, the wild Kentucky frontiersmen supplied it. They were fearless, cocky settlers, haters of Indians, already the victims and the aggressors as well in much bloody border warfare. Their plan was to break up the budding confederacy before it could gain any more strength. Even before the negotiators met at Fort Harmar, the frontiersmen had been sending raiding parties into Indian territory. Naturally, the Indians struck back. By the time winter came in 1789, the new nation was headed for an Indian war that it did not want.

President Washington had hoped to avoid trouble, since the nation needed all the peace it could obtain to shape its future. However, he could hardly ignore what was happening in the Ohio Valley. Between the end of the Revolution and October, 1790, nearly fifteen hundred men, women, and children had been killed, wounded, or taken prisoner along the Ohio and its tributaries. The Indians had also stolen at least two thousand horses from the settlers, and they had taken other property amounting to about fifty thousand dollars.

Washington was a man of incredible patience, but even his endurance came to an end in April, 1790. One of his emissaries, a Major Doughty, on his way to visit the Chickasaws on government business, encountered four canoes loaded with Shawnees and Cherokees paddling the other way on the Tennessee River. Doughty and his fifteen men took the Indians aboard when they displayed a white flag, and gave them presents. The parting was friendly. But when the canoes were back in the river again, the Indians raised their guns and poured a volley into the boat, killing or wounding eleven men.

Now Washington knew he must move, and move quickly. There was another reason for speed. The news from Europe said that England and Spain might go to war. If that occurred, the Mississippi River itself could become a war highway between the British forts in the north and the Spanish forts in the south, with all that might mean in further stirring up the tribes.

General Harmar's Expedition

Major General Arthur St. Clair, governor of the Northwest Territory, arrived in New York City late in August, 1790. He hastened to meet Washington at the President's house — the new government had not yet moved to Philadelphia — and the two discussed what ought to be done about defending the frontier.

St. Clair was a Scot who had fought with the British in Canada during the French and Indian War. He had liked the New World so well that he bought himself four thousand acres of land in western Pennsylvania when the war was over and settled down as the largest resident property-owner in the state west of the Alleghenies. During the Revolution he had fought in Canada again, this time with the Americans, and later joined Washington in the battles of Trenton and Princeton. There was a shadow on his military career, however. Ordered to defend Fort Ticonderoga in 1777, a position everyone thought impregnable, St. Clair had evacuated it without a fight, for which he was court-martialed. The court exonerated him, but he was given no other important military duties. As governor of the Northwest Territory, he had not been particularly skillful in dealing with the Indians.

But it was the Indians he had come to talk about with Washington. Early that spring, a particularly troublesome band had been making raids from their village on the north bank of the Ohio. Every effort to make peace with them had failed. It was Washington's opinion, shared by his Secretary of War, Henry Knox, the former Boston bookseller who had been Washington's general of artillery in the Revolution, that a short, vigorous campaign was needed to punish the Indians and perhaps set an example to other tribes.

The President had instructed St. Clair to assemble the expedition, and in July the governor had begun to requisition the necessary militia. About fifteen hundred raw, untrained men were assembling at Fort Washington, where the city of Cincinnati now stands, ready to march in the early autumn. They were under the command of a man whom Washington did not know personally. He had been appointed by St. Clair.

Brevet Brigadier General Josiah Harmar had fought with the Pennsylvania troops during the Revolution, but was now rumored to be a heavy drinker. To Harmar's command, St. Clair had added some three hundred professional Federal soldiers and six hundred Kentucky militiamen, who were enthusiastic enough but lacked discipline and training.

It was the plans for Harmar's campaign that St. Clair and President Washington discussed in the quiet rooms of Number 3 Cherry Street, in New York. Washington realized that St. Clair had never experienced frontier warfare himself — something the President knew a great deal about because of his own hard and sometimes disastrous youthful experiences as a colonel of the Virginia militia. Consequently, he took pains to warn St. Clair about the dangers of handling troops in the wilderness. There was one rule above all others to remember, he said: "Always beware of surprise."

St. Clair served with Washington, shown above at the Battle of Trenton.

Major General Arthur St. Clair. (Charles Phelps Cushing)

Armed with this and other good advice, St. Clair went home, where he found Harmar nearly ready to begin his advance. The ill-assorted little army marched out of Fort Washington in September, 1790. Meanwhile, the Indians had ample warning of its coming. St. Clair had thought it a good idea to inform the British garrison at Detroit that the expedition was not aimed against it, a piece of information swiftly passed on to the Indian allies of the English—just what Washington feared would happen when he heard what St. Clair had done.

Back in New York, the President fretted through the long autumn weeks. No news of Harmar's progress, or lack of it, came from the West. All Washington heard was the rumor about Harmar's love of the bottle, and that was not very reassuring. Grimly, Washington instructed Knox to prepare a statement for Congress describing why the campaign had been undertaken. If the disaster he feared took place, the President knew that Congress would be asking him sharp questions.

His fears were justified. Harmar had marched straight into defeat. As his army advanced, the Indians slowly retreated, drawing the white men deeper into their territory. At one point an advance scouting party of 210 men caught up with their quarry. The outnumbered red men turned around and set on them with such ferocity that the inexperienced militiamen fled in panic. The regulars who stayed to fight were nearly cut off.

After this skirmish, the Indians resumed their retreat. Harmar regrouped his forces and followed them once more. Not far from the chief village of the Miamis, on the site of what is now Fort Wayne, Indiana, the Indians turned again and fell on Harmar's men with their full strength. When it was over, 183 of the invaders lay dead. At that, it was not as bad a defeat as it could have been. Thanks

Josiah Harmar marched his troops straight to defeat.
(Charles Phelps Cushing)

to the valor of the regulars, the Indians lost enough men to prevent a complete massacre of Harmar's unfortunate army. The survivors were able to leave the field, carrying their dead and wounded.

That simple fact of survival was enough to enable Harmar to represent the whole affair as a victory when he made his report. Washington and Knox, old soldiers as they were, knew better. They themselves escaped criticism for the defeat because they had kept Congress informed and had made no effort to hide the facts. Harmar was not so fortunate.

Voices were raised in Congress demanding to know what had happened and asking for a court of inquiry. The court was duly convened, and Harmar appeared before it to tell his story. Astonishing as it might seem in the light of historical fact, the court not only vindicated him but declared that he ought to be given "high approbation" rather than censure. A little more than a year later, however, Harmar resigned his commission.

St. Clair Takes the Field

Following his conference with Washington in New York, St. Clair had presented the President with a plan of his own to bring the situation in the Ohio Valley under control. He proposed to assemble an army at Fort Washington and march 135 miles northward to the chief Miami village of KeKionaga. There St. Clair intended to build a fort large enough and strong enough to intimidate all the Indians for miles around, at the same time letting the British know that the Americans had no intention of giving up the Ohio Valley to the king.

At first, this plan was rejected. Knox thought it was beyond the still-slim military resources of the new nation. But the more he discussed it with Washington, the better it seemed, particularly after news of what had happened to Harmar reached the capital. Clearly, something had to be done about the Indians, and St. Clair's plan offered what seemed to be a sensible approach.

The plan was sensible, it is true, but seldom has a military enterprise been so badly planned and carried out, although it began with considerable flourish. In March of 1791, St. Clair was given back the rank of major general he had held in the army during the Revolution. That made him the ranking officer in the peacetime army; the regulars had no other major general. Next, the commander got his orders from the President, and they were clear enough: he was to "establish a strong and permanent military post" where the Miami capital had been and, after it was constructed and garrisoned, he was to "seek the enemy" and "endeavor by all possible means to strike them with great severity." This is comparable to the "search-and-destroy" strategy used in Vietnam in our time.

Those were the orders. Unfortunately, St. Clair was not capable of carrying them out. He was superbly unprepared for what he was commissioned to do. As he gathered his army of less than three thousand men at Fort Washington in the early summer of 1791, the whole problem of what to do with the Indians was still being hotly debated in Philadelphia, where the government had moved from New York. There were those who argued that all the trouble in the Ohio Valley would end as soon as the United States could settle its differences with England about the disputed frontier posts. The difficulties with the Creeks in the South would be over, too, it was said, if Spain could be persuaded to make the commanders in its Florida forts stop supplying the Indians with guns and powder.

There was a difference of opinion at the highest level. President Washington's policy was to do everything he could to strengthen the ties with friendly tribes and, meanwhile, hammer into submission any Indian nation that resisted the government. St. Clair's campaign was to be a part of that policy. But Washington's Secretary of State, Thomas Jefferson, wanted to take a harder line toward the Indians — what might be called a "law-and-order" policy today. The first order of business, he said, was to give all the Indians a "thorough drubbing." After that, they could be pacified with "liberal and repeated presents."

It was not that Washington loved or trusted the Indians any

more than did his Secretary of State. The President simply believed that the Indian problem would never be solved permanently unless a firm peace could be made with them. The secret of making that peace, he also believed, was to prevent the settlers from encroaching on lands that were Indian property.

Washington understood what lay at the heart of the Indian problem, but his priorities were wrong. If an honest attempt to prevent encroachment had ever been made, the oncoming tragedy in the Ohio Valley might have been avoided. As it was, the plan to subdue the resisting tribes first and seek peace afterward was mistaken. Of course, Washington did not realize that matters would turn out that way. Somehow, he imagined that St. Clair would build his forts, as proposed, and that this would cement old alliances and intimidate the other Indians without bloodshed.

Never was a policy conceived with so little real reason for optimism. Because of St. Clair's utter incompetence, the seeds of disaster were well sown before the army ever marched away. His troops were badly armed and poorly equipped. Moreover, nearly two-thirds of them were militia. As they moved into the field, St. Clair began to have the same difficulties with them that had plagued Washington throughout the Revolution and had caused him to lash out angrily at the militiamen more than once. One of the chief difficulties with these drafted soldiers during the war had been their determination to leave the service the moment their term of enlistment ended — even if it was just before an important battle or at any other time when their departure might make a serious difference.

St. Clair's militia began to leave in trickles as their enlistments ended, while others simply deserted. However, they did have one legitimate complaint. Money for the expedition was slow in coming from Philadelphia, and the soldiers' regular monthly pay of three

Washington felt that a firm peace must be established with the Indians. (The Bettmann Archive)

dollars seldom arrived. Aside from that, the militia were terrified at the prospect of fighting the Indians. They were also indignant at the idea of doing such nonmilitary chores as building forts, especially when the food began to run as low as the money — another result of St. Clair's bad planning.

Nothing seemed to go well. The expedition had been scheduled to leave Fort Washington in July, but St. Clair had been so slow about getting it in motion that it was autumn before the march began. By that time the early frosts had reduced the grass to a brown carpet, and this was the only source of food for horses and cattle. St. Clair had made no other plan for provisioning his animals.

The march was agonizingly slow. Not only was the army unable to move rapidly because it lacked proper supplies, but St. Clair had orders to withhold any offensive action until the government's agent, Thomas Proctor, had made one more attempt to make peace with the tribes. The attempt failed, like the others.

As the gloomy November days drew on, St. Clair's force of three thousand had dwindled to fourteen hundred. The only thing its commander had to show for his efforts was a few small and inadequate forts built along the way.

On the afternoon of November 3, this army — in one sense already beaten — camped on one of the upper tributaries of the Wabash River, one hundred miles north of Fort Washington. Morale in the camp that day was extremely low, not only among the men but among the officers as well. The more experienced of them were now aware that their commander was incompetent. He had refused to take any of their advice, even ignoring the counsel of his second in command, General Richard Butler, who was much more familiar with frontier warfare.

What horrified Butler and the other experienced officers was St. Clair's failure to send out scouts ahead of the army. The commander had no idea of the size of the Indian force he was supposed to fight; he did not even have any precise idea of where it was.

Little Turtle's Campaign

If St. Clair had learned the essential facts about his enemy, he would have had good reason to be alarmed. The leader of the Miamis, and commander of the Indian army now opposing the white invaders, was one of the most important chiefs in the Northwest Territory, a master of war strategy and a great orator. Little Turtle's Indian name was Michikinikwa. Born about 1752 in a Miami village on the Eel River, some twenty miles from the leading Miami town, he was the son of a chief. That, however, did him little good. His mother was a Mohican and, according to Indian custom, he was considered a member of her tribe. But he was such an outstanding young man that, even without the help of his father's position, he was soon made a chief of the Miamis.

From his early days, Little Turtle had been a friend of the British. He had helped their cause during the Revolution and, in the troubled years after it was over, he had remained loyal as the dispute over the frontier forts developed. He was no friend of the Americans; they were, after all, the people who were busy taking over the land where his tribe had lived for uncounted moons.

Little Turtle's scouts kept him well informed about St. Clair's advance. They would have had little fault to find with the campsite

Little Turtle, the great chief of the Miamis. (The Bettmann Archive)

In the thick of battle. (Charles Phelps Cushing)

he had chosen on the third of November. It was on high ground, behind a creek. The artillery had been placed in the center of the camp, with the militia stationed on the other side of the stream, where they spent the afternoon flushing out Indian scouts from the underbrush. They did not know it, but they were already surrounded by Little Turtle's warriors.

About half an hour before a misty November sun could penetrate the forest the next morning, the troops in the main camp were just being dismissed from the usual inspection which began their day, when there was a burst of firing on the other side of the creek, where the militia were stationed. In a moment the water was filled with splashing, terrified men, utterly disorganized. They stormed across the stream into camp, where they milled around among the regulars, causing a fatal delay before St. Clair could form his ranks. It was the old story of raw, untrained militia troops under fire, many of them for the first time.

Little Turtle took full advantage of the confusion in the American camp. Quickly he surrounded it, and St. Clair's army was doomed. Not only had this incompetent commander ignored Washington's warning that he must at all costs avoid surprise but he also now repeated the familiar mistake that had cost regular troops, both British and American, so many lives in their encounters with Indians. Like the British regulars under General Edward Braddock in the massacre that young Colonel Washington remembered with such horror for so many years, St. Clair's troops stood in the ranks they had formed. Completely exposed, they were slaughtered by the Indians, who fired from behind cover and were almost impossible to hit.

There was no lack of bravery in St. Clair's army. The men stood up to the withering fire of the Indians, like Braddock's soldiers, and they even counterattacked with great courage when they were ordered. But it was obvious they were going to be killed to the last man if they stood their ground. It took three hours of fighting before St. Clair understood this fact, and only then did he order a retreat.

In justice to St. Clair, it must be noted that he had been very ill before the battle, and could not even get on or off his horse without help. Under the circumstances, he did his best to organize a proper retreat, but not until a ruinous amount of damage had been done. Nor did St. Clair attempt to put his departure from the field in a better light. "It was, in fact, a flight," he wrote bluntly in his report. And at that, he was lucky. The Indians pursued them for several miles and, if they had chosen to do so, could have killed every one of the 580 survivors they permitted to reach safety.

American forces had seldom suffered such a complete, humiliating defeat. The total casualties were more than nine hundred men. All the artillery was lost, along with most of the other equipment, which had to be abandoned.

"The most disgraceful part of the business," St. Clair wrote, "is that the greatest part of the men threw away their arms and accoutrements, even after the pursuit . . . had ceased. I found the road strewed with them for many miles. . . ."

President Washington's Defense

The first news of the disaster reached the government indirectly, by way of a letter from Shippensburg, Pennsylvania, printed in *Dunlap's American Daily Advertiser*, one of the best of the Philadelphia newspapers. The next day other newspapers in the city carried another report of the battle that had come from Kentucky by way of Richmond, Virginia. Washington undoubtedly read these reports, but he had to wait until the night of December 9 before he got St. Clair's own dispatches, which were sent first to Secretary Knox and then passed on to the President.

How Washington got these dispatches, and how he received them, make an entertaining legend that has persisted for more than a century. Years later, in the published reminiscences of men who were trying to remember what they had seen or been told long before, it was said that St. Clair's exhausted messenger had arrived by night and refused to give his dispatches to anyone but Washington. When the President was roused and read the reports, according to the story, he went into a towering rage, stomped up and down the room, and swore at St. Clair.

While it was true that Washington had a temper he had to fight to control for a good part of his life, in this case the facts were

otherwise. What happened was that St. Clair's messenger arrived early in the evening at a time when the President was entertaining guests. Moreover, since it was a Friday night, he was due to appear shortly at Mrs. Washington's usual reception held on that day. He had only time to take a quick look at the dispatches, but the opening words must have been enough to make him feel sick with dismay and arouse him to anger.

"Yesterday afternoon," St. Clair wrote, "the remains of the army under my command got back to this place [Fort Washington], and I now have the painful task to give you an account of as warm and as unfortunate an action as almost any that has been fought, in which every corps was engaged and worsted, except the First Regiment. That had been detached. . . ."

With the iron control that was one of his most useful characteristics, Washington got through the evening in his customary reserved, dignified fashion and bowed the last guest out of the house before he returned to reading the dispatches. St. Clair had made no attempt to conceal anything. As Washington read on, the worst unfolded — the dead stacked up around the cannon, the persistence with which these guns were fed until there was no longer anyone alive who knew how to do it, the gradual beating down of the American forces into a bloody, disorganized mass, the final charge that cleared the road for retreat, the utter panic that gripped the men as the Indians pursued them, and the terror and hunger with which they staggered on all night toward the safety of Fort Washington.

The engraving on pages 32-33 shows one of Martha Washington's Friday night receptions. (Library of Congress)

There was a postscript in which St. Clair noted, in his own defense, that "some very material intelligence" had been given by Captain Jacob Slough to General Butler on the night before the battle. But this information had never been passed on to him, and he had not known about it until well after the defeat. Slough, it turned out, had made a reconnaissance when the army pitched camp and had discovered that the woods around the site were full of Indians. But when Slough reported this to Butler and urged that he be permitted to inform St. Clair at once, Butler persuaded him to rest and promised to convey the information himself. He did not do so. Why? Washington would never know, because Butler was dead, shot down with the others. And the President knew that he himself would not escape criticism for Butler's negligence, because he had appointed the man to this command over the protests of those who had argued that he was not qualified.

So Washington could have been excused if he used strong words and gave vent to his temper after he read the report and its postscript, and no doubt he did, although not to the extent reported in the legend. Congress had adjourned for the weekend, so he had two days to think of how best to inform them. When he wrote his brief message, probably sitting at his desk in the beautiful home of his old friend, Robert Morris, on Market Street — the President's official residence for the moment — he was as frank and uncompromising as St. Clair had been in his report.

"Gentlemen of the Senate and of the House of Representatives," Washington wrote. "It is with great concern that I communicate to you the information received from Major General St. Clair, of the misfortune which has befallen the troops under his command. Although the national loss is considerable, according to the scale of the event, yet it may be repaired without great difficulty, excepting as to the brave men who have fallen on the occasion, and who are a subject of public as well as private regret. A further communication will shortly be made of all such matters as shall be necessary to enable the Legislature to judge of the future measures which it may be proper to pursue."

Attached to this message were copies of St. Clair's reports, with all the humiliating details. Washington well knew that the people trusted him. They did so because he trusted *them* and was absolutely honest with them even when it would have been politically advantageous to gloss over or evade the truth. He instructed Knox to prepare a series of further reports which would tell in detail everything that had been done to placate the Indians and get their support. One of these reports also told the Congress, in unsparing detail, what it would cost the new nation in men and money if they meant to make the frontiers secure.

Congress Takes Action

Not even such honesty, of course, was enough to stifle criticism. Congress insisted on an inquiry. The newspapers, especially those hostile to the administration, were full of letters from readers criticizing the event in various ways. One of them, Benjamin Franklin Bache's *General Advertiser*, a stern critic of Washington's, raised the question of whether the United States had any right to invade the Indians' lands — especially when it was proving to be so expensive. In other papers, the President and Secretary Knox were both attacked and defended.

Throughout this storm, Washington himself was not blamed, and Knox rather less than he expected to be. Even St. Clair drew more sympathy than censure. People were inclined to blame mostly the army contractors who had failed to supply St. Clair's army properly, and they were also concerned about such larger and more impersonal questions as the best way to fight Indians, and whether it was ethical to occupy Indian territory at all. Washington's honesty, apparently, kept the whole affair from becoming a political issue.

As for St. Clair, he asked for a court of inquiry to clear himself of blame for the defeat. However, Washington could not authorize one, because, for the moment, there were no other officers in the

Washington and his Cabinet, which includes Henry Knox (next to the President), Alexander Hamilton, Thomas Jefferson, and Edmund Randolph. (The Bettmann Archive)

army of high-enough rank to sit on a court and judge a major general, according to law. St. Clair then resigned his commission. But when the House of Representatives ordered its own investigation of the affair, St. Clair changed his mind and asked to retain his rank until the inquiry was over. Washington told him that only one major general was permitted in the army, and an officer of that rank was needed in the field. Later, a congressional committee inexplicably declared St. Clair innocent of all blame for the disaster, in spite of all the evidence to the contrary. That offended Knox, who argued that this verdict amounted to a censure of him (Knox), but another inquiry, convened at the secretary's request, upheld the first committee.

One result of the controversy was a renewed demand for peace with the Indians. An army was created large enough to do the job of enforcing it. New officers were appointed: Anthony Wayne as the ranking major general, and four new brigadier generals. Congress also passed a law which gave the President the right to call out the militia for purposes of executing laws, suppressing insurrections, and repelling invasions.

Anthony Wayne Takes Command

While these activities were going on, the victorious Indians of the Ohio Valley were being encouraged by their British friends who were pressing harder than ever for control of the frontier states and a buffer state. The Indians had no particular interest in a buffer state. They were talking about driving all the American settlers out of the lands north of the Ohio River. By 1792 their raids were ousting farmers from lands on the Allegheny, Muskingum, and Great Miami rivers. The fugitive survivors of these raids were seeking shelter in Wheeling, Pittsburgh, and Louisville; fortified places like those at Cincinnati and Marietta were now the only safe outposts.

The displaced settlers cried out for relief, criticism of the government began to rise, and Washington responded in every way he could. The President still hoped for peace, and his agents were working hard to bring it about, although there seemed little hope for it. Meanwhile, the fresh army, under its new commander, Anthony Wayne, was forming on the banks of the Ohio River above Pittsburgh, at a settlement called Legionville. Wayne called his budding army "the Legion."

Wayne's unfortunate nickname — Mad Anthony — is the one that clings to him even today. In fact, he was anything but mad,

General Anthony Wayne. (The Bettmann Archive)

"*Mad Anthony*" *won his nickname for his daring attack at Stony Point, New York, 1779.*

and the more familiar title that his men gave him — "Old Tony" — was much more fitting. For Wayne was essentially a conservative man. "Mad Anthony" had been the admiring popular name given him when his light infantry surprised the garrison at Stony Point on a July night in 1779. He captured this most northerly British outpost on the Hudson River, along with nearly seven hundred men, fifteen cannon, and valuable stores. Congress gave him a medal for that feat, and the happy patriots gave him the nickname that endured.

But it was "Old Tony" and not "Mad Anthony" who settled down on a rice plantation in Georgia after the war. The state had given him the land in recognition of his service with General Nathanael Greene in the long year after Yorktown, when the British still held out in Charleston and the irreconcilable Creek Indians were still terrorizing the Georgia countryside. Wayne routed the Indians and negotiated treaties of submission with them.

Back in civilian life, he still talked like a military man. He had a great contempt for states like Pennsylvania which had fashioned a liberal constitution as an outcome of the revolt against Great Britain. He called the makers of this constitution "radicals" and the document itself "not worth defending."

As commander of the Legion, Wayne was against Washington's peace maneuvers with the Indians. He was for organizing the army and getting on with the job of beating the tribes into submission, which he considered the task that the government had given him to accomplish. This time there would be no repetition of St. Clair's supply troubles. Messengers kept the trails warm between Legionville and the capital with an exchange of messages between Wayne and Washington and Knox, most of them having to do with provisioning and preparing the army.

[44]

General Nathanael Greene. (Charles Phelps Cushing)

Meanwhile, Washington did not give up his hopes for peaceful negotiation. Five agents had been sent out to Indian country during 1792. Only one had come back with a formal agreement, and this was with unimportant chiefs of the Wabash and Illinois tribes. The government was also trying to use the influence of Joseph Brant, the powerful chief of the Six Nations. By the end of 1792, Brant, heading a delegation from the northern tribes, had succeeded in arranging a call to a peace conference.

These peacemakers from the Six Nations came to visit the President in February of 1793. They hinted that the hostile tribes might be willing to negotiate for a boundary on the Ohio River. The President selected his best negotiators from those men who were willing to venture among the "hostile" tribes. A cabinet meeting agreed that they should be empowered to make any concessions that were "essential to peace."

A Council Leads to War

As progress toward a great council with the Indians of the Northwest went forward, it seemed to Washington that as fast as he moved to stem trouble in one quarter, it burst out in another. By April there was new unrest in the South, where agents of the Spanish and English alike were busy stirring up trouble. The Creeks were increasingly hostile and the Seminoles were frequently on the war-path. When they were not fighting their old enemies, the Creeks, the Chickasaws were making raids against the white settlers. From Georgia to Virginia to Tennessee to the Ohio came reports of unrest and raids. The new nation had no frontier it could call friendly.

The only ray of hope now was the forthcoming conference with the Indians, to take place at Sandusky, Ohio. So much depended on the outcome that both Knox and Washington went to extraordinary lengths to prevent any incident that might upset the negotiations. There was to be a kind of collective holding of the breath along the northwestern frontier until the council was over.

St. Clair, who was still governor, had his instructions from Knox in April: "The President . . . has particularly directed me to inform you that the proposed treaty with the hostile Indians . . . will be held at Lower Sandusky about the 1st of June. . . . During the continuance of the treaty [he meant the negotiations] it is of the highest importance . . . that all hostile incursions of the white inhabitants into or near to the Indian Country . . . should be absolutely prohibited. . . . The President requests that you . . . take such measures in the premises with your frontier citizens as shall in your judgment be most effectual to prevent a measure which might be attended with highly pernicious consequences."

Wayne had similar instructions. There was always the danger that angry frontiersmen whose homes had been burned or families killed would descend on an Indian town in revenge. Even though their actions might seem justified to them, the chances for peace could disappear.

Meanwhile, Wayne put his Legion in a position to keep the peace, if necessary, and placed himself in readiness for a campaign, if that was how events turned. With his army he left Legionville on April 29 and sailed down the Ohio, floating past Fort McIntosh, Wheeling, Marietta, Gallipolis, and Limestone. He finally made camp on safe ground not far from Cincinnati, at a place called Hobson's Choice.

Just about the time that Wayne was navigating the Ohio, two of Washington's three chosen commissioners were setting out for Sandusky. Timothy Pickering and Beverly Randolph headed first for Niagara, where a British vessel was to take them across Lake Erie. The third man, Benjamin Lincoln, had gone before them with the baggage and stores for the expedition. Jefferson watched them depart with little optimism. He termed the approaching conference "this last effort for living in peace with the Indians."

Even Jefferson, who expected so little, was shocked by what actually occurred. The conference had been scheduled for the early part of June, but the three commissioners never reached Sandusky. When they got to Niagara, Lieutenant Governor John Simcoe of

Lieutenant Governor John Simcoe introduces his family to his Indian allies.
(Charles Phelps Cushing)

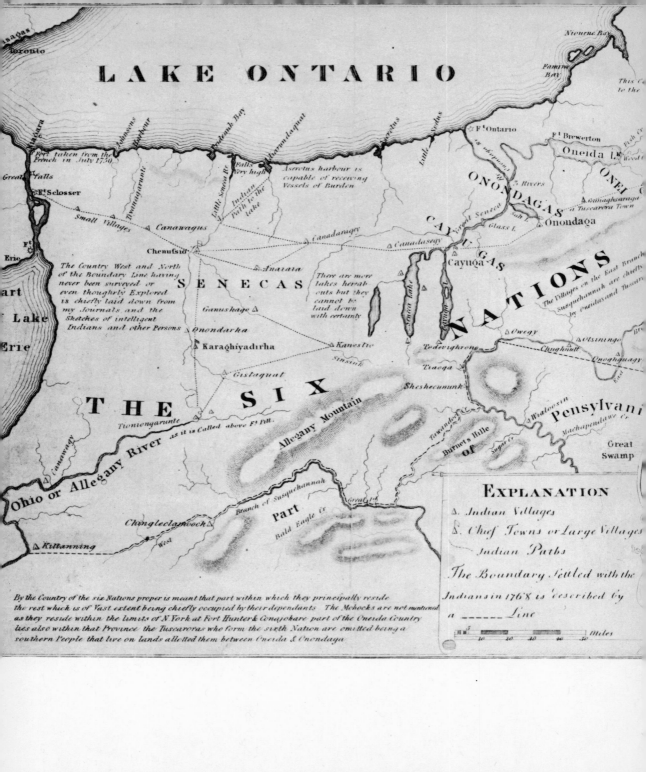

LAKE ONTARIO

Niourne Bay

Famine Bay

This Co to the

Toronto

Fort taken from the French in July 1750.

Johnsons Harbour

Ft Ontario

Ft Brewerton

Fish Cr

Oneida Lk

Wood Cr

ONEI

Great Falls

Ft Slosser

Pwatnagunati

Little Seneca Rr

Falls very high

Indian Path to the lake

Irondaquat

Asertus harbour is capable of receiving Vessels of Burden

3 Rivers

ONONDAGAS

Suttaghsaraga a Tuscarora Town

Ft Erie

Small Villages

Canawagus

Canadarager

Canadasegy

Great Seneca

Sub L

Glass L.

Onondaga

CAYUGAS

art of Lake Erie

Chenufsio

Anaiaia

There are more lakes herabouts but they cannot be laid down with certainty

Cayuga

Seneca Lake

NATIONS

The Villages on the East Branch of Susquehannah are chiefly by Oneida and Tuscarora

SENECAS

The Country West and North of the Boundary Line having never been surveyed or even thoughtly Explored is chiefly laid down from my Journals and the Sketches of intelligent Indians and other Persons

Ganushage

Cayuga Lake

Owegy

Otsiningo

Chughnutt

Onoghquagr

Karaghiyadirha

Kanestio

Todevighrone

East

Cistaquat

Sinsink

Traoqa

Sheshecununk

THE **SIX**

Tioniongarunte

Allegany Mountain

Tawandee

Burnets Hille

Wateosin

PENSYLVANI

Machapendawe Cr

Ohio or Allegany River as it is Called above Ft Pitt.

Sugar Cr

Great Swamp

Canawagy

Part **of**

Branch of Susquehannah

Bald Eagle Cr

Great Isl

Chingleclamooch

West

Kittanning

EXPLANATION

△ Indian Villages

▲ Chief Towns or Large Villages

Indian Paths

The Boundary Settled with the Indians in 1768 is described by a ——— Line

10   20   30   40   50   Miles

By the Country of the six Nations proper is meant that part within which they principally reside the rest which is of Vast extent being chiefly occupied by their dependants   The Mohocks are not mentioned as they reside within the limits of N.York at Fort Hunter & Conajohare part of the Oneida Country lies also within that Province the Tuscaroras who form the sixth Nation are omitted being a southern People that live on lands allotted them between Oneida & Onondaga

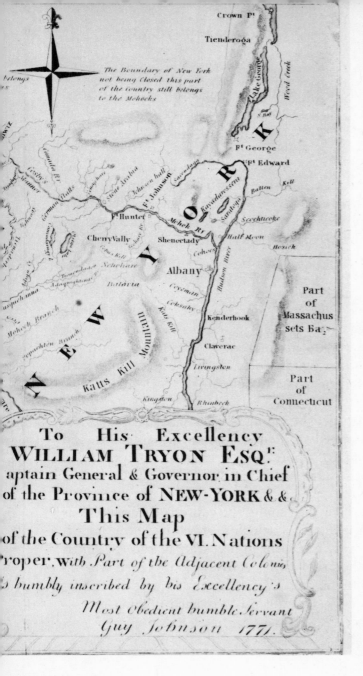

Eighteenth-century map showing territory occupied by Indians of the Six Nations. (Charles Phelps Cushing)

Canada did not provide them with the immediate transportation across the lake that they had expected. Instead, he detained them for seven weeks with the excuse that the Indians had told him they were not yet ready for negotiation.

At last Simcoe had the commissioners taken to a place on the Canadian shore of Lake Erie, about eighteen miles below Detroit. There they were told flatly that they could proceed no farther. They were obliged to take quarters on the farm of a British officer named Matthew Elliott, who arranged for several chiefs to visit them there on July 31.

The chiefs demanded that the frontier revert to the old boundary on the Ohio River, according to the agreement at Fort Stanwix in 1768. There was no point, of course, in even discussing this proposal. The frustrated commissioners stayed two weeks more with Captain Elliott, unable even to make arrangements to talk with the Indians again. The most the chiefs would do was to send a written message, repeating their proposal, this time in the form of an ultimatum.

Disgusted and heartsick, the commissioners packed up and left for home. Randolph stopped at Mount Vernon in September and gave Washington a detailed report. The President was sorely disappointed but not surprised. He had long believed that the Canadians would do everything they could to create trouble on the northwest border, and he blamed them for ruining the conference. Still, it was a hard blow. The great council for which so much had been hoped, and for which months had been spent in preparation, had amounted to no more than two hours of futile conversation. There was no other course left. It had to be war. Wayne was told that the negotiations were a failure — he had confidently expected nothing else — and was advised to proceed.

Wayne Begins His March

The restless and impetuous Wayne received the words he had been waiting for. His three thousand men of the Legion began to march on October 7, 1793. They followed the same route that St. Clair had taken and, ironically, Wayne began to experience some of his predecessor's troubles. A quick Indian raid deprived him of some supply wagons and horses; there was reluctance and even near mutiny among the militia.

But Wayne was a far different commander than St. Clair had been. He got matters in hand, and the army moved twice as fast as had the troops of 1791. Wayne decided to make winter camp north of Cincinnati. He erected a stockade called Fort Greeneville in honor of his wartime commander, the brilliant, limping General Nathanael Greene.

Washington heard about the loss of the horses and the supply wagons and the mutinous troops, but he did not lose confidence in Wayne. This was going to be the best he could do — this final, great thrust of a large army. It was also the most he could do to protect the settlers on the northwest frontier and secure the Ohio Valley against the Indians and the British. If Anthony Wayne, the hero of Stony Point, was unequal to the task, then Washington felt he could do no more. He hoped Wayne would be able to strike out against the Miamis in a winter campaign, but the general preferred to wait until spring.

It was an uneasy interval. Wayne had to contend with the familiar problems of desertions and the departures of militia when their enlistments expired. He also experienced the less familiar problem of quelling sedition among the officers, who found Wayne a harsher commander than they liked. In Philadelphia, Washington had to contend with criticism of what seemed like inaction on the part of his western commander. One critic complained to Jefferson that Wayne seemed to be "a man of very moderate abilities, vain, capricious, jealous in the extreme, a dupe to the few who flatter him."

Thus, the difficult winter passed, while Washington dealt with the thousand and one other problems that beset him. Then, in May, alarming news reached Philadelphia. It was reported that Lieutenant Governor Simcoe, apparently believing that Wayne was on his way to attack Detroit (or at least pretending he thought so), had sent three companies of British soldiers to reactivate Fort Miamis, sixty miles southward. This was the outpost that the British had previously abandoned. It stood at the rapids of the Maumee, not far from where the Legion was encamped, and Simcoe's seizure of the fort was an invasion of American territory. Indignant words flew between London and Philadelphia, and Philadelphia and Quebec.

There was an American provocation, too. Late in May, Governor Thomas Mifflin of Pennsylvania ordered a thousand militia sent to Presque Isle, a town on the eastern edge of Lake Erie. Mifflin did not inform the President. Washington feared that Simcoe would interpret Mifflin's move as a challenge to his troops at Fort Miamis, even though Mifflin apparently meant it as protection for the settlers who were surveying and occupying land there under the auspices of

Thomas Mifflin, governor of Pennsylvania. (The Bettmann Archive)

the state. Fortunately, when the Pennsylvania governor heard about the President's fears, he withdrew his orders, although reluctantly. Washington knew that the settlers Mifflin meant to protect might protest, but he would rather have their criticism than a further inducement to war with England.

Little Turtle's Downfall

While these maneuvers were going on, Wayne continued to drill his troops methodically, instructing them how to fight Indians. No doubt he could hear the voice of Knox in his ears: "Let it therefore be again, and for the last time impressed deeply upon your mind, that a defeat at the present time, and under the present circumstances, would be ruinous to the interests of our country." Knox had written these words the previous September, and Wayne had replied: "You may rest assured that I will not commit the Legion unnecessarily."

Even in the winter snows, Wayne did not sit by idly, waiting for events to develop. Besides the constant drilling and instruction of the troops, he sent a detachment of them up the river to the place of St. Clair's defeat. He gave a decent burial to the remains of those who had fallen, and over their graves built a fort aptly named Recovery.

Wayne soon had the Indians in a state of anxiety. Wise as he was, Little Turtle was led into a serious error. It was not entirely his fault: he was the victim of events taking place on the great world stage, far removed from the Ohio Valley. England had entered into war against the French revolutionists during the winter. Because the

British were seriously interfering with American shipping as a result, the United States was threatening to enter the war on the side of France.

At the height of the tension between the two nations, the governor of Quebec, Lord Dorchester, told a visiting delegation of western chiefs that war could not be avoided. Then he told the chiefs what they most wanted to hear. When the war came, he said, the British would fight side by side with the Indians and restore the hunting grounds that the Americans had taken from them. That was why Simcoe had sent his soldiers from Detroit to reactivate Fort Miamis, and it was why Little Turtle made his error.

The chief had the utmost respect for Wayne, whom he understood was a far different kind of commander than Harmar or St. Clair. He had already advised his tribesmen that it might be better to make peace with this "chief who never sleeps." They did not listen. Now that their white father in Canada had assured them that they and their British brothers were about to regain the power they had lost, nothing could have held them back.

Little Turtle had no choice but to lead them, against his better judgment. He could have isolated Wayne where he was, surrounding him and waiting for him to try to break out, when presumably he would have met St. Clair's fate. Instead, the expectant, joyful Indians gathered two thousand strong at Fort Miamis late in June. They attacked Fort Recovery, driving a small American scouting party ahead of them. There was a brief, sharp battle, and the Indians retreated with heavy losses. A good many were so discouraged that they went home.

English faces had been seen among the besiegers of the fort. So, Wayne redoubled his efforts, after the battle, to convince the English that he had no quarrel with them on this campaign, and that Detroit and the other British outposts would be safe. He did not tell them that Secretary Knox had been so pleased with the defense of Fort Recovery that Wayne had been authorized, in the name of the President of the United States, to "dislodge" the English garrison in their fort at the rapids of the Maumee.

Wayne's efforts with the British must have had some effect, because Little Turtle found it difficult to get any support from his supposed allies. They were ready to urge on the red men into battle, and they furnished a few supplies, but they were plainly reluctant to commit any men. Little Turtle saw the way the wind was blowing, and he began once more to urge his warriors and lesser chiefs to make peace with the Americans. But although he was a powerful orator, the other chiefs would not listen. They sat around, boasting of their past successes, talking of the help they would get from the British, and vowing revenge for what had happened to them at Fort Recovery.

Part of Little Turtle's difficulty could be laid to his personality. He was not an easy man to get along with and had never been really popular with many of the chiefs. Six feet tall, usually unsmiling — even sullen — arrogant and arbitrary in his manner, he tended to look down upon the others as inferior men, which in truth they were. Even worse, he had been friendly with the white men — far too friendly, the other chiefs thought — and he had taken on some of the white man's ways. When he led the warriors into battle with St. Clair's army, he wore deerskin leggings and moccasins, in the approved way, but with a blue petticoat falling halfway down his thighs and a European waistcoat. The Indian cap on his head was decorated with more than two hundred silver brooches, reaching halfway down his back. Two rings hung from each ear. The upper part of each one was made of three silver medals the size of a dollar,

An Indian village, this one belonging to the Mohawks, around the time of the Battle of Fallen Timbers. (Charles Phelps Cushing)

the lower part of each the size of a quarter. These creations fell twelve inches from his ears, it was said. In his nose he wore three jewels "of wonderful pattern."

Whether or not this legend was true, there is no doubt that Little Turtle's fellow chiefs were jealous of him. When he advised them to make peace, they took advantage of the unpopularity of this idea among the tribes and brought so much pressure against their leader that he lost his high place in the council and his role as war chief. This vengeance was not only poor payment for the many victories Little Turtle had won for them and his wise counsel in other matters, but it also deprived them of the one man who could have saved them.

Of course, the other chiefs did not know that. They simply replaced Little Turtle with a chief they liked better, Turkey Foot, who did not have his predecessor's extraordinary talents.

Turkey Foot soon found that Little Turtle had been right about one thing. The British showed no intention of contributing any substantial number of troops to the army that the Indians were assembling at Fort Miamis. There were only a few Canadian militia and volunteers mingling with the two thousand warriors, who boasted and danced and lounged about the great Indian village.

The Battle of Fallen Timbers

Meanwhile, events were drawing rapidly to a climax, after so many years of waiting and preparation on both sides. The showdown for control of the Ohio Valley was near. Wayne was cheered tremendously, early in July of 1794, when a large body of Kentucky volunteers appeared. Kentuckians might be difficult disciplinary problems to a commander, but they were fearless and obsessed with hatred of the Indians, no doubt because they had suffered more from raiding parties than had other settlers.

With this reinforcement, Wayne ordered the advance at last. The columns of the Legion, now nearly three thousand strong, began to move through the forest along the Auglaize River, heading northward. At the point where the Auglaize flowed into the Maumee, he built another strongpoint, which he named Fort Defiance. There, too, Wayne paused long enough to inquire by messenger if the Indians had any desire to make peace. They did not. They considered themselves ready for a decisive battle, and were eager for it.

Moving again, but cautiously now, the Legion advanced down the Maumee. Dim shapes of Indians could be seen just ahead of the advance patrols, and occasionally the two forces came together lightly as the patrolling forces on both sides touched. Turkey Foot

THE BATTLE OF
FALLEN TIMBERS

Miles

0   50   100

ATLANTIC OCEAN

Montréal

Ft. Point-au-Fer
Ft. Dutchman's Point
L. Champlain
VT.
Ft. George

St. Lawrence R.
Ft. Oswegatchie

Hudson R.

Albany
Kingston
New York
Trenton
NEW JERSEY
Delaware R.
New Castle
DELAWARE

Mohawk R.
Ft. Stanwix
Ft. Oswego

NEW YORK

Wilkes-Barre
Susquehanna R.
Reading
Harris' Ferry (Harrisburg)
Lancaster
Philadelphia
York
MARYLAND
Baltimore
Annapolis
Washington
Alexandria
Potomac R.

FINGER LAKES

IROQUOIS INDIANS

Ft. Niagara
Buffalo

LAKE ONTARIO

ALLEGHENY MOUNTAINS

PENNSYLVANIA

Ft. Ligonier
Shippensburg
Ft. Cumberland

VIRGINIA

Presque Isle (Erie)

Allegheny R.
Pittsburgh
Ft. McIntosh
Wheeling

LAKE ERIE

Georgian Bay

LAKE HURON

Cleveland
Ft. Sandusky
CONN. RESERVE
Ft. Lawrence
DELAWARE INDIANS

WYANDOT
SHAWNEE INDIANS

Ft. Miamis
Ft. Defiance

Marietta
Ft. Harmar
Ohio R.
Zanesville
Muskingum R.
Trace
Zane's Trace
(OHIO)
Franklington (Columbus)
Chillicothe
Scioto R.
Gallipolis
Ohio R.

FALLEN TIMBERS (1794)

Ft. Mackinac

Ft. Detroit

(MICHIGAN)

C a n a d a

Northwest Territory

MIAMIS INDIANS
Harmar's Defeat (1791)
Kekionaga Village

Maumee R.
Ft. Wayne
Ft. Recovery
Ft. Loramie
Ft. Greenville
Ft. Washington (Cincinnati)
HARMAR
ST. CLAIR
WAYNE
Great Miami R.
Little Miami R.

Eel R.
Wabash R.
Mississinewa R.
St. Clair's Defeat (1790)

(INDIANA)

KENTUCKY

Limestone (Mayville)
Louisville

N

and his warriors fell back slowly before Wayne's advance, until at
last they came to a piece of terrain they considered ideal for battle.

The site was called Fallen Timbers. Once a tornado had swept
through the forest there, throwing the trees around in wild abandon
until they made a thick tangle of fallen trunks and limbs. Turkey
Foot meant to spread his warriors through this impenetrable tangle,
which would give them enough cover and make them almost impossible to dislodge.

Wayne, in his later report, acknowledged that Turkey Foot
had chosen well. The nature of this battleground, he wrote, "ren-
dered it impracticable for cavalry to act with effect, and afforded
the enemy the most favorable covert for their savage mode of warfare." It was also favorable in other ways. The Indians were pro-
tected on their left flank by the Maumee. Not far to the rear stood
the stockades of Fort Miamis, the British stronghold which had done
so much to cause the trouble in the first place. Turkey Foot planned
to fall back on the fort if he had no other choice.

Arriving at the scene and seeing how well Turkey Foot had
disposed himself, Wayne showed what a master of Indian warfare
he had become. Turkey Foot expected him to mount some kind of
assault at once; this was the way the white men had always fought.
Instead, Wayne waited, without making a move . . . one day . . .
two days . . . three days. The Indians, who had not supplied themselves with food — they thought the battle would soon be over —
began to grow hungry. Some retired a little way to find provisions
or to hunt a little, to fill their bellies. Those who remained were
impatient and ravenously hungry.

On the morning of August 20, the Indians could wait no longer.
A strong force was sent out from the shelter of the fallen timbers
and fell upon Wayne's advance guard. They were repulsed. Sensing

that the time had come, the general gave the warriors no time to reorganize.)He sent his Kentucky volunteer cavalry to attack the Indian right. Then he hurled his main force at the center, using the tactics he had worked out and spent all winter rehearsing. Wayne tells the story well in his official report:

"I ordered the front line to advance with trailed arms," he writes, "rouse the Indians from their coverts at the point of the bayonet and, when up, to deliver a close and well directed fire on their backs followed by a brisk charge so as not to give time to load again. . . . Such was the impetuosity of the charge by the first line of infantry that the Indians and Canadian militia and volunteers were driven from all their coverts in so short a time that, although every exertion was used by the officers of the second line of the Legion, and by Generals Scott, Todd, and Barber of the Mounted Volunteers to gain their proper positions, yet but a part of each could get up in season to participate in the action, the enemy being driven in the course of an hour more than two miles through the thick woods already mentioned by less than one half of their numbers. . . . From every acount the enemy amounted to two thousand combatants, and the troops actually engaged against them were short of nine hundred."

In brief, Wayne had won without even committing the bulk of his army. Nor was that the worst of it, from the Indians' standpoint. Not only had they been driven from what had seemed an impregnable position, and been outsmarted at their own game, but when Turkey Foot led the retreat, with Wayne's troops in hot pursuit, and tried to carry out his previous plan of seeking shelter in Fort Miamis, the British commander refused to open the gates to him. The Indians stood outside, clamoring to get in, while Wayne's men cut them down without mercy.

It was one of the worst disasters ever suffered by Indians in their centuries-long struggle with the white men. Wayne lost only thirty-eight men, and another hundred or so wounded. As usual, the Indians did not say how many of their number were killed, but it could only have been tragically great.

Wayne was in no mood to reward the British for their cruel and treacherous cooperation. The next day he and some of his staff officers rode out on a reconnoitering expedition, so close to Fort Miamis that the commander could not help seeing them. He sent Wayne an indignant note, demanding to know what the American general was up to. "It becomes my duty," the commander said, and one could almost hear the snort behind the words, "to inform myself as speedily as possible in what light I am to view your making such near approaches to this garrison."

The answer from Wayne might have been written from one of his revolutionary headquarters: "Without questioning the . . . propriety, Sir, of your interrogatory, I . . . may . . . observe to you that were you entitled to an answer, the most full and satisfactory one was announced to you from the muzzles of my small arms yesterday morning in the actions against the hordes of savages in the vicinity of your post. . . . But had it continued until the Indians *etc* had been driven under the influence of the post and guns you mention they would not have much impeded the progress of the Victorious Army under my command. . . ."

Having put the British commander in his place, Wayne fell back with his army to Fort Defiance. There they rested for a week or two. Then came the final devastating blow to the Indian tribes. Wayne led his army to the site of their villages, where Harmar had been defeated in the early days of the war, and methodically began to destroy everything in sight. He burned the villages to the ground

The Battle of Fallen Timbers. (Charles Phelps Cushing)

and laid waste more than five thousand acres of the land where they grew their crops.

Then Wayne sent a message to the defeated chiefs. Their cause was hopeless, he told them — certainly they could see that for themselves. This being so, they might as well sign a really conclusive treaty of peace with the Americans. The President had sent his messenger (that would be John Jay) to London, and he had secured a treaty of peace at last between America and England. Consequently, the Indians could expect no more help of any kind from the British. Without that help, Wayne concluded persuasively and accurately, the red men had no hope of winning out against the American government.

The Treaty of Greenville

The chiefs agreed; they had no other choice. On August 3, 1795, eleven hundred Indian chiefs and warriors met the American peace commissioners at Fort Greeneville (or "Greenville," as it came to be known; General Greene's name was persistently misspelled), ready to negotiate the treaty prepared for them. There was little to negotiate, in fact. The Indians had no alternative but to accept what was offered. Nevertheless, to save face, and following their custom, they spent days making long speeches. Their main arguments were that they had never intended to damage their American friends and that the evil British had pushed them into actions they could now see were wrong. Beneath the words ran a pathetic plea for simple justice, to be allowed to hunt and live on the lands they had occupied for centuries.

But there was no justice when the Americans were dealing with the Indians, the original owners of the land. They did not concede a single point in the treaty or give the Indians the slightest hope.

Wayne read the treaty to them for the last time. When he was finished, he asked, "Do you approve these articles?" One by one the chiefs of the tribe stood up to answer, tall and short, sullen or remote, but all of them with a bearing of quiet dignity. They were humbled but unconquered. The only answer — "Yes" — came from the lips of Ottawas, Potawatomis, Wyandots, Delawares, Shawnees, Miamis, Chippewas, Kickapoos, Weas, Piankashaws, and Kaskaskias.

An officer on Wayne's staff sketched this solemn, sad ceremony. Today it can be seen at the Chicago Historical Society. There stands Wayne, proud and tall, with his epaulets, surrounded by his officers, including William Henry Harrison, who would one day become the ninth President of the United States. Wayne had cited him for bravery during the campaign. Chief Little Turtle, who had not led his people in war at Fallen Timbers but now was their leader at the peace conference, stands to the right of the American officers, speaking to them with eloquent gestures. Behind him is Tark the Crane, a noted chief of the Wyandots.

Missing in the picture, among the Indian chiefs with Little Turtle, is the man who was probably the most important Indian at the gathering. He had fought at Fallen Timbers with his brothers. He was a Shawnee chief named Tecumseh, meaning "Crouching Tiger" in the Indian tongue. Like Little Turtle, Tecumseh was an extraordinary Indian, sometimes called the greatest one who ever lived. On his shoulders was to fall the leadership of the tribes. It was he who would lead them back to fight another great war with the white men on another day.

For the moment, however, there was only Little Turtle, and he was the last to sign the treaty. It would have been understandable if he had paused one more moment before he signed, for he well knew what the Indians were giving away. It was nothing less than a territory so large that today it comprises the whole state of Ohio and a part of Indiana.

Nevertheless, he signed it, accepting the inevitable. But in his heart, and in the hearts of the other tribesmen, was a bitter hatred

Chief Tecumseh.
(Charles Phelps Cushing)

of the British who had betrayed them, and an even more savage, frustrated rage against the Americans who had destroyed their homes and crops, and were now taking their lands. Little Turtle did not believe any of the promises contained in the treaty — he knew all about the white man's treaties. But, forlornly, he sought to give evidence of his own good faith.

"I am the last to sign it," he said, taking up the quill, "and I will be the last to break it."

Besides the land given up, the tribes had granted reservations of different sizes surrounding Fort Wayne, Fort Defiance, and Detroit. Whatever land remained was magnanimously recognized by the United States as belonging to the Indians. When the treaty was ratified, the government passed out twenty thousand dollars' worth of presents to the Indians — somewhat in the manner of giving lollipops to children for being good. The government also agreed to pay certain annuities to the tribes, but these payments did not last long. As for the British forts, which had caused the trouble, Jay's treaty finally compelled the British to turn them over to the Americans, twelve years after the Revolution had supposedly ended English control of them. A year after the Battle of Fallen Timbers, Wayne returned to the Northwest to receive the surrender of these posts.

With that act, the drama that had begun with the Treaty of 1783 came to an end. The Treaty of Greenville had been the final speech of the players. Indian resistance in the Old Northwest had ended, and it would never be quite so threatening again, even under Tecumseh's leadership. The alliance between the British and the Indians, which had caused so much mischief, was broken, and would not be renewed again until the War of 1812. Most important, from the standpoint of the American government, a new and fertile area had been cleared and made reasonably safe for settlement by the people of the expanding new nation.

The actors left the stage. Victorious General Wayne had not long to live. Before he could reach home again, after he had received the surrender of the British forts, he died on the way, at Presque Isle (now Erie, Pennsylvania) on December 15, 1796.

St. Clair had a longer career ahead of him. He continued to govern the Northwest Territory, but his manner of doing it so irritated the Jeffersonians that in 1801 they started a movement to get him out of office, while at the same time they hoped to create the state of Ohio. They were successful in getting Congress to admit the state, but they had no luck ousting St. Clair. However, he committed political suicide by denouncing the act that had made Ohio a state, whereupon Jefferson himself removed the governor from office.

After that, St. Clair went into retirement at the Hermitage, his home near Ligonier, Pennsylvania. Among other things, he constructed an iron furnace capable of making stoves and castings. But he was always a man who was the victim of his own personality, and one of the traits that endeared him to his friends ultimately ruined him. He lent money freely to them and gladly signed their notes, which he often had to redeem. Morover, there was a new administration in power now, a Republican one, and it shamefully refused to repay St. Clair, the Federalist ex-governor, for the money he had spent out of his own pocket on the nation's business while he was governor. As a result, he lost his entire fortune, slipped into poverty and oblivion, and died in the log cabin on Chestnut Ridge that became his last home.

Of all the actors, Little Turtle fared best. He lived to sign many other treaties with the United States on behalf of his tribesmen, and the older he grew, the closer he came to the white men. Eventually the United States gave him a special annuity of his own. He even acquired a white son-in-law. In 1805, the government raised his annuity by fifty dollars and gave him a slave.

GEORGE WASHINGTON
PRESIDENT 1795

Medal commemorating the Greenville treaty, 1795, in which the Indians were forced to sign away their land and rights. (Charles Phelps Cushing)

As the scene of the Indian Wars moved westward, Little Turtle traveled a great deal through the East. He visited the growing cities, and became a kind of "tame Indian," an object of great curiosity and even admiration for thousands of Americans — almost a living folk hero. He was entertained in the best places, and met important men, including the French philosopher, Volney, and the Polish hero Kosciusko, who gave him some splendid gifts.

Still an orator of great eloquence and much in demand as a speaker at the white men's banquets, he gave a memorable speech in Baltimore in 1801 before a committee of Friends, in which he denounced the introduction of whiskey into Indian country.

Naturally, as he drew closer to the white men, his influence with his own people declined. However, for a long time he was able to act as a go-between, respected if not always trusted by both sides. He kept his tribe, the Miamis, out of Tecumseh's confederacy. Nevertheless, there were Indian prophets who predicted darkly that in the end the white men would ruin him.

They were correct, in an odd way. In the house that the government had built for him in his village, Little Turtle lived so well and so lazily that he acquired a white man's disease — gout. The army surgeon at Fort Wayne treated him, but he died of complications from the disease on July 14, 1812, as the United States found itself locked once more in a struggle with England. The western forts and the western Indians were again pawns between the two great forces.

As for the Treaty of Greenville, it was broken over and over again like all the other treaties the American government made with the Indians. Another treaty signed at almost the same time with the Senecas remained as the oldest Indian treaty in this century. It bore the name of George Washington as one of the signers. In the 1960's, it was finally broken for good when the Kinzua Dam was built on the Allegheny River. The waters that were backed up behind the dam flooded the ancestral lands of the Senecas who still lived there. Even though the Senecas received compensation for their loss, they were nevertheless driven from their homes. General Wayne could not have planned it better.

Selected Bibliography

Billington, Ray Allen. *Westward Expansion*. New York: Macmillan, 1960.

Dictionary of American Biography (for biographies of Generals Harmar, St. Clair, and Wayne, and of Little Turtle). New York: Scribner's, 1928.

Freeman, Douglas Southall. *George Washington*, vols. VI and VII. New York: Scribner's, 1954 and 1957.

Pageant of America. New Haven: Yale University Press, 1929.

Tebbel, John (with Keith Jennison). *The American Indian Wars*. New York: Harper, 1960.

———. *Compact History of the Indian Wars*. New York: Hawthorn Books, 1966.

Index

Allegheny River, 41, 71
Auglaize River, 63

Bache, Benjamin Franklin, 37
Barber, General (Mounted Volunteers), 66
Braddock, General Edward, 29
Brant, Joseph (Mohawk chief), 8, 11, 46
Butler, General Richard, 24-25, 35

Cherokee Indians, 11
Chicago Historical Society, 72
Chickasaw Indians, 11, 47
Chippewa Indians, 8, 72
Cincinnati (Ohio), 41, 48, 53
    see also Fort Washington
Creek Indians, 21, 44, 47

Delaware Indians, 8, 72
Dorchester, Lord (governor of Quebec), 58
Doughty, Major, 11-12
Dunlap's American Daily Advertiser (Philadelphia), 31

Eel River, 26
Elliott, Matthew, 52
England. *See* Great Britain
Erie (Presque Isle), Pennsylvania, 54, 75

Fallen Timbers, Battle of, 63-70
Federalist party, 75
Fort Defiance, 63, 67, 74
Fort Greeneville, 53
    treaty signed at, 71-79
Fort Harmar, 11
Fort Miamis: British troops at, 54-56, 58, 59, 65, 66, 67
    Indian army at, 62
Fort Recovery, 57
    Little Turtle's attack on, 58-59
Fort Stanwix, agreement at (1768), 52
Fort Washington, 14, 17, 34
    St. Clair and, 20, 21, 24
    see also Cincinnati
Fort Wayne (Indiana), 17, 74, 78
France, and Great Britain (wars with), 13, 57-58
French and Indian War, 13
Fur posts. *See* Northwest fur posts

General Advertiser (newspaper), 37
Great Britain: and France (wars with), 13, 57-58
    and Indian allies, 17, 26, 40, 47, 58-59, 62, 66-67, 70, 71, 74
    and Jay's treaty, 70, 74
    and Northwest fur posts, 5-12, 21, 26, 74
    and Revolutionary War, 3, 44

and Spain (war with), 12
troops of (*see:* Fort Miamis;
    Simcoe, Lieutenant Governor
    John)
and War of 1812, 74, 78
Great Miami River, 41
Greene, General Nathanael, 44, 53, 71
Greenville, Treaty of, 71-79
"Greenville." *See* Fort Greeneville

Haldimand, Governor-General Frederick, 6, 8
Harmar, General Josiah, 14-19, 20, 58,
67
Harrison, William Henry, 72
Hobson's Choice, Wayne's camp at,
48

Illinois Indians, 46
Indian confederacy, 8-12
see also Brant, Joseph
Iroquois Indians, 5, 8

Jay, John, treaty with Great Britain
of, 70, 74
Jefferson, Thomas (Secretary of
State), 21-22, 48, 54, 75
Johnson, Sir John, 8

Kaskaskia Indians, 72
KeKionaga (Miami village), 20, 21,
26
Kentucky, settlers from, 11, 14, 63, 66
Kickapoo Indians, 8, 72
Kinzua Dam (Allegheny River), 79
Knox, Henry (Secretary of War):

and Harmar, 14, 17, 19
and St. Clair, 20, 31, 36, 37, 40
and Sandusky conference, 47-48
and Wayne, 44-46, 57, 59
Kosciusko, Thaddeus, 78

"Legion, The," 41, 44, 48, 57
and Battle of Fallen Timbers, 63-
70
march of, 53-54
see also Wayne, General Anthony
Legionville, 41, 44, 48•
Lincoln, Benjamin, 48-52
Little Turtle (Miami chief): campaign of, 26-30
defeat of, 57-62
after Fallen Timbers, 75-78
and Greenville Treaty, 72-74

"Mad Anthony" nickname explained,
41-44
see also Wayne, General Anthony
Marietta (Ohio), 41, 48
Maumee River, 54, 59
and Battle of Fallen Timbers, 63-
70
see also Fort Miamis
Miami Indians, 8, 17, 20, 72
chiefs of (*see:* Little Turtle, Turkey Foot)
chief town of (*see* KeKionaga)
Wayne against (*see* Wayne, General Anthony)
Michikinikwa. *See* Little Turtle
Mifflin, Governor Thomas (Pennsylvania), 54-56

Mohawk Indians, 8
    chief of (*see* Brant, Joseph)
Mohican Indians, 26
Morris, Robert, 35
Mounted Volunteers, 66
Muskingum River, 41

Northwest fur posts, 5-12, 21, 26
    in Jay's treaty, 74
Northwest Ordinance (1787), 5

Ohio, statehood for, 75
Ottawa Indians, 8, 72

Piankashaw Indians, 72
Pickering, Timothy, 48-52
Pittsburgh, Pennsylvania, 41
Potawatomi Indians, 8, 72
Presque Isle (Erie), Pennsylvania, 54, 75
Proctor, Thomas, 24

Randolph, Beverly, 48-52
Republican party (Jeffersonian), 75
Revolutionary War, Great Britain
    and, 3, 44
    treaty ending, 3, 5, 6, 74
    see also Yorktown, Battle of

St. Clair, Major General Arthur, 11, 29, 58
    defeat of, 31-36, 37-40, 44, 57
    expedition of, 20-25, 53
    as governor of Northwest Territory, 5, 75
    and Harmar's expedition, 13-17

and Little Turtle, 26-30, 59
and Sandusky conference, 47-48
and Washington, 13-16, 20, 21, 26, 31-36, 41
Sandusky (Ohio), Indian conference at, 47-52
Scott, General (Mounted Volunteers), 66
"Search-and-destroy" strategy, 21
Seneca Indians, 8
    U.S. treaty with, 78-79
Shawnee Indians, 8, 11, 72
    see also Tecumseh (Shawnee chief)
Simcoe, Lieutenant Governor John (Canada), 48-52, 54, 58
    see also Fort Miamis, British troops at
Six Nations, 46
    see also Brant, Joseph
Slough, Captain Jacob, 35
Spain: and Great Britain (war with), 12
    and Southern Indians, 21, 47

Tark the Crane (Wyandot chief), 72
Tecumseh (Shawnee chief), 72, 74, 78
Todd, General (Mounted Volunteers), 66
Treaty of Greenville, 71-79
Treaty of 1783, 3, 5, 6, 74
Turkey Foot (Miami chief), 62
    and Battle of Fallen Timbers, 63-70

U.S. Congress: and Ohio statehood, 75
    and St. Clair's defeat, 35-36, 37-40
    and Wayne (medal for), 43

Volney (French philosopher), 78

Wabash Indians, 46
Wabash River, 24
War of 1812, 74, 78
Washington, President George, 3
    and Harmar, 13-19
    Indian policies of, 10-12, 21-22, 78
    Indians' view of, 5
    and Jay's treaty, 70, 74
    opponents of, 37
    and St. Clair, 13-16, 20, 21, 26, 31-36, 41

    and Sandusky conference, 47-52
    and Wayne, 44-46, 53-56, 59
Washington, Mrs. George, 34
Wayne, General Anthony, 74, 75, 79
    army of (see "Legion, The")
    assumes command, 40, 41-46
    background of, 41-44
    and Battle of Fallen Timbers, 63-70
    and Greenville Treaty, 71-75
    and Little Turtle, 57-59
    march of, 53-54
    nicknames explained, 41-44
    and Sandusky conference, 48, 52
    and Washington, 44-46, 53-56, 59
Wea Indians, 72
Wheeling (West Virginia), 41, 48
Wyandot Indians, 8, 72

Yorktown, Battle of (1781), 3, 44

[86]

About the Author

Born in Michigan and now a resident of New York City, John Tebbel was educated at Central Michigan College and Columbia University. He is the author of several books, including *The American Indian Wars*. An experienced journalist, he has been a writer for *Newsweek* magazine and a Sunday staff writer for *The New York Times*. At present the author is chairman of the department of journalism at New York University. *The Battle of Fallen Timbers* is his first book for Franklin Watts, Inc.